COOKING
FOR TWO

Rhona Newman

GOLDEN PRESS / NEW YORK
Western Publishing Company, Inc.
Racine, Wisconsin

CONTENTS

This edition published 1984 by Golden Press
Library of Congress Catalog Card Number: 84-80337
ISBN 0-307-09966-0
Golden® and Golden Press® are registered trademarks
of Western Publishing Company, Inc.

First published in 1980 in the U.K. by Cathay Books,
59 Grosvenor Street, London W1

© 1984, 1983, 1980 Cathay Books

Printed in Hong Kong

This edition prepared
under the supervision
of Joanna Morris

INTRODUCTION

Here is a wonderfully inventive cookbook, truly tailored for two. Now each new day can bring a new adventure in eating with these specially designed nutritious, attractive dishes. You'll find recipes for all occasions, from quick snack lunches to intimate dinner parties for two.

While some recipes do make excellent use of those inevitable leftovers, you'll discover that the emphasis here is on fresh foods, freshly prepared.

Most of these dishes are quick and easy to make; others may require a little planning. Whatever the occasion, whatever your schedule, this practical cookbook will provide pleasure and inspiration when cooking for two.

NOTES:

Unless otherwise noted, all recipes in this book serve two.

Always preheat the oven to the specified temperature.

Margarine can be substituted for butter in all recipes.

If substituting dried herbs for fresh, use a third of the amount; if substituting fresh for dried, use 3 times the amount.

BREAKFASTS

Tangy Grapefruit

1 grapefruit, cut in half

2 to 4 tablespoons raisins

¼ cup plain yogurt

1 to 2 tablespoons brown sugar (optional)

Cut out the segments from each grapefruit half, discarding the pith and membranes and reserving the shells. Place the segments in a small bowl and stir in the raisins and yogurt.

Spoon the mixture into the shells and sprinkle with the sugar. Refrigerate until ready to serve.

Bananas with Yogurt

1 banana, sliced
1 cup vanilla yogurt
2 tablespoons
   chopped nuts
2 tablespoons bran
   or wheat germ

Divide the banana slices between two bowls. Top with yogurt and sprinkle with the nuts and bran.

Muesli

½ cup plain granola
¼ cup grapenuts
   cereal
2 tablespoons raisins
1 tablespoon brown
   sugar
2 tablespoons
   toasted almonds
Milk

Put the cereals, raisins, sugar and nuts in a bowl. Mix well and divide between 2 cereal dishes. Add milk when ready to serve.

Cereal Mix

2 zwieback, crushed
1 cup cornflakes
3 tablespoons bran
  cereal
1 apple, peeled and
  grated
2 teaspoons brown
  sugar
2 tablespoons fruit
  yogurt
Milk

Put all ingredients except the yogurt and milk into a bowl. Mix well, then divide between 2 cereal dishes. Spoon the yogurt on top and add milk to serve.

Orange Eggnog

1½ cups cold milk
1 egg
2 tablespoons lemon
   yogurt
Grated rind and juice
   of 1 orange
1 teaspoon honey
Grated nutmeg

Beat the milk with the egg. Add the yogurt, orange rind, juice and honey and beat until well blended.

Pour into glasses and serve, sprinkled with nutmeg.

Sardine Toast

1 can (3¼ oz)
   sardines, drained
1 tablespoon butter
Grated rind and juice
   of 1 lemon
1 tablespoon
   chopped parsley
Pepper
2 slices whole wheat
   bread, toasted

Place the sardines in a small shallow pan, dot with butter and broil until hot and bubbly.

Transfer the fish to a bowl and mash with a fork. Add the lemon rind and juice, parsley and pepper to taste and mix well. Spread the mixture over the toast.

Brown lightly under a preheated broiler for 3 to 4 minutes. Serve immediately. Garnish with parsley sprigs if desired.

Bean Bonanza

1 can (8 oz) pork and
   beans
1 hard-cooked egg,
   chopped
½ cup chopped
   cooked ham
1 teaspoon
   Worcestershire
   sauce
1 teaspoon prepared
   mustard
1 tablespoon
   ketchup
Salt and pepper
2 slices bread,
   toasted
1 tablespoon butter

Put the beans in a small saucepan with the egg, ham, Worcestershire sauce, mustard and ketchup. Heat gently; add salt and pepper to taste.

Spread the toast with the butter and spoon the bean mixture on top. Serve immediately.

10

Sunrise Scramble

3 eggs
2 tablespoons
   half-and-half
Salt and pepper
2 tablespoons butter
½ small onion,
   finely chopped
1 tomato, chopped
2 slices bread,
   toasted

Beat the eggs with the half-and-half and season with salt and pepper.

Melt half the butter in a small skillet, add the onion and sauté until soft. Pour in the egg mixture and cook slowly over low heat, stirring until scrambled. Stir in the tomato and remove from heat.

Spread the toast with the remaining butter and spoon the eggs on top. Serve immediately.

Cheese-Topped Muffins

1 tablespoon butter
1 cup grated Cheddar
 cheese
½ teaspoon Dijon
 mustard
1 teaspoon milk
Salt and pepper
2 English muffins
4 slices tomato

Melt the butter in a small saucepan and add the cheese. Cook over low heat, stirring, until the cheese is melted. Stir in the mustard and milk and season with salt and pepper.

Split the muffins in half and toast. Spread with the cheese mixture and top with tomato slices. Place under a preheated broiler for 2 to 3 minutes until heated through and the cheese is bubbling. Serve immediately. Garnish with parsley if desired.

Bacon-Wrapped Sausages

4 pork sausage links
Prepared hot
 mustard
4 thin strips Cheddar
 cheese
2 slices bacon, cut in
 half

Broil the sausages under a preheated broiler for 6 to 8 minutes, turning to brown evenly. Spread with mustard.

Place a strip of cheese on each sausage, then wrap with bacon. Return to the broiler for an additional 6 to 8 minutes, turning once. Serve with broiled tomatoes or baked beans; or put the sausages in toasted frankfurter rolls for a lunch dish.

MEAT & POULTRY

Steaks with Béarnaise

2 tablespoons wine
  vinegar
2 tablespoons dry
  white wine
1 teaspoon minced
  shallots or green
  onions
½ teaspoon dried
  tarragon
1 egg yolk
1 teaspoon cold
  water
4 tablespoons butter,
  at room
  temperature
Salt and pepper
2 beef steaks, about
  1 inch thick
1 tablespoon oil

Combine the vinegar, wine, shallots and tarragon in a small saucepan and cook down to 2 teaspoons; do not brown.

Whisk the egg yolk in a small metal bowl until light in color. Beat in the cold water. Place the bowl over (not touching) very hot water and beat the butter in gradually with a whisk. When the sauce thickens, add salt and pepper to taste. Keep the sauce in a warm place while preparing the steaks.

Season the steaks with salt and pepper to taste. Heat the oil in a skillet and sauté the steaks from 3 to 5 minutes on each side, according to the degree of doneness desired. Serve topped with sauce, or serve the sauce on the side.

Beef Rouladen

2 slices bacon, halved and partially cooked
4 thin slices beef round (⅛ inch thick)
½ dill pickle, cut into 4 wedges
½ carrot, cut into julienne strips
¼ onion, cut into julienne strips
Seasoned flour
2 tablespoons oil
½ cup beef broth
½ cup dry red wine
1 tablespoon tomato paste
2 tablespoons chopped shallots
2 teaspoons cornstarch

Place a piece of bacon in the center of each beef slice; top with a wedge of pickle and a few carrot and onion slivers. Roll and secure each with a wooden pick.

Dredge the rolls in the flour; heat the oil in a skillet and brown the rolls. Transfer to a shallow baking dish large enough to hold the rolls in a single layer.

Discard any fat in the skillet and add the broth, wine, tomato paste and shallots. Bring to a boil, scraping the pan, and pour over the rouladen. Cover and bake in a 350° oven for 1½ hours.

Transfer the rouladen to a warmed platter. Dissolve the cornstarch in 2 tablespoons water and add to the sauce, boiling until thickened. Pour the sauce over the rouladen and serve.

Beef with Orange

1½ tablespoons
 flour
Salt and pepper
¾ lb beef chuck
 steak, cubed
1 tablespoon butter
1 small onion,
 chopped
½ green pepper,
 seeded and
 chopped
Grated rind and juice
 of 1 orange
1 cup beef stock or
 broth

Season the flour with salt and pepper and coat the meat. Melt the butter in a small skillet, add the onion and green pepper and sauté until soft. Add the meat and brown on all sides. Transfer to a 1-quart casserole.

Stir in the orange rind, juice and stock and season with salt and pepper. Cover and bake in a 325° oven for 1 to 1¼ hours, or until the meat is tender. Serve piping hot, garnished with chopped parsley if desired.

Beef and Cheddar Bake

½ lb lean ground beef
1 small onion, finely chopped
1 stalk celery, chopped
¼ cup chopped mushrooms
1 small carrot, grated
1 teaspoon flour
⅔ cup beef stock or broth
½ teaspoon Worcestershire sauce
Salt and pepper
TOPPING:
¾ cup whole wheat flour
3 tablespoons oatmeal
2 tablespoons butter
⅓ cup grated Cheddar cheese
½ teaspoon dried mixed herbs

Brown the beef in a small skillet, crumbling it in the process. Add the onion, celery, mushrooms and carrot and cook over low heat for 5 minutes. Stir in the flour and cook for 1 minute. Add the stock and Worcestershire sauce and season with salt and pepper. Bring to a boil, stirring. Cover and simmer for 30 to 40 minutes.

TOPPING: Combine the flour and oatmeal in a bowl and cut in the butter until the mixture resembles coarse bread crumbs. Stir in the cheese and herbs and season with salt and pepper.

Transfer the meat mixture to a greased small baking dish and spoon the topping over it. Bake in a 375° oven for 20 to 30 minutes. Garnish with parsley if desired.

Chili con Carne

¼ cup dried red
   kidney beans
¾ lb lean ground
   beef
1 onion, finely
   chopped
½ small green
   pepper, seeded and
   chopped
1 can (8 oz) tomatoes
2 tablespoons water
1 teaspoon chili
   powder
½ teaspoon cumin
   seeds
Salt and pepper

Place the beans in a bowl and cover with cold water; soak overnight. Drain the beans, rinse and place in a small saucepan. Cover with fresh cold water. Bring to a boil and boil for 10 minutes. Lower the heat and simmer for 25 minutes; drain.

Brown the beef in a skillet until it is crumbly. Add the onion and green pepper and sauté for 5 minutes. Stir in the tomatoes with their juice, water, chili powder and cumin.

Bring to a boil, stirring, then add the beans. Cover and simmer for 1 hour, or until the beans are tender. Season with salt and pepper to taste.

Serve hot in warmed bowls. Accompany with a green salad and pita bread if desired.

Broiled Hamburgers with Barbecue Sauce

SAUCE:
1 tablespoon butter
1 onion, finely
  chopped
1 tablespoon ketchup
1 tablespoon vinegar
1 tablespoon brown
  sugar
Pinch of chili
  powder
½ teaspoon dry
  mustard
½ teaspoon dried
  mixed herbs
6 tablespoons water
HAMBURGERS:
½ lb lean ground
  beef
2 teaspoons finely
  chopped onion
½ teaspoon prepared
  mustard
2 teaspoons chopped
  parsley
1 tablespoon butter,
  melted

SAUCE: Melt butter in a small sauce-pan; add the onion and sauté until soft. Combine the remaining sauce ingredients and add to the pan. Bring to a boil, cover and simmer for 20 minutes.
HAMBURGERS: While the sauce is cooking, put the ground beef, onion, mustard and parsley in a bowl. Season with salt and pepper and mix well. Shape the mixture into 4 patties.

Brush the patties with the melted butter and broil to desired degree of doneness, turning once.

Transfer to a warmed serving dish and pass the sauce separately. French fries and green beans or peas are delicious accompaniments.

Lamb Steak with Mustard Butter

½ to 1 teaspoon
  Dijon mustard
2 tablespoons butter
1 or 2 lamb leg
  steaks, about 1 lb
  total
Salt and pepper
1 tablespoon oil
¼ cup dry white
  wine or chicken
  broth

Cream the mustard with the butter until fluffy; set aside. Season the steak with salt and pepper. Heat the oil in a skillet and sauté the steak for 3 to 5 minutes on each side, according to the degree of doneness desired. Remove the steak to a warmed platter.

Discard any oil in the pan and add the wine. Bring to a boil, scraping the pan, and reduce until almost a syrup. Swirl in the flavored butter a tablespoon at a time. Pour the sauce over the steak and serve.

NOTE: The flavored butter can be made in a larger quantity and stored in the refrigerator. It must be re-softened before each use. The butter is also delicious on beef steaks.

Lamb Stew

2 large potatoes,
  thinly sliced
1 lb trimmed cubed
  stewing lamb
Salt and pepper
1 onion, sliced
2 carrots, sliced
1 stalk celery,
  chopped
½ teaspoon dried
  thyme
1 cup stock or broth
1 tablespoon butter,
  melted

Cover the bottom of a 1-quart casserole with half the potatoes. Arrange the lamb on top and season with salt and pepper.

Combine the sliced onion, carrots and celery; season with the thyme and additional salt and pepper. Spread over the lamb and add the stock. Arrange the remaining potatoes in overlapping circles on top and brush with the melted butter.

Cover and bake in a 350° oven for 1½ hours. Remove cover and continue to bake an additional 20 to 30 minutes, or until the potatoes are lightly browned.

Pork and Apple Casserole

1 tablespoon oil or
  butter
1 small onion, sliced
1 clove garlic,
  crushed
¾ lb boneless pork
  cubes
2 teaspoons flour
⅔ cup cider
3 tablespoons stock
  or broth
½ teaspoon dried
  sage
Salt and pepper
1 large apple, peeled,
  cored and sliced
2 tablespoons light
  cream

Put the oil in a skillet, add the onion and garlic and sauté until soft. Add the pork and brown on all sides. With a slotted spoon, transfer the mixture to a 1-quart casserole.

Add the flour to the skillet and cook for 1 minute. Gradually stir in the cider and stock and cook, stirring, until the sauce thickens.

Stir in the sage and add salt and pepper to taste. Arrange the apple slices over the pork in the casserole and pour the sauce over all. Cover and bake in a 350° oven for 1½ hours.

Gently stir in the cream. Serve garnished with chopped parsley if desired.

Pork with Prunes

1 tablespoon flour
Salt and pepper
2 boneless pork
  chops, about
  ¾ inch thick
1 tablespoon butter
1 teaspoon oil
⅔ cup cider
6 large pitted prunes
1 teaspoon lemon
  juice
2 teaspoons currant
  jelly
¼ cup heavy cream

Season the flour with salt and pepper and toss with the meat. Heat the butter and oil in a skillet. Add the chops and cook for 5 minutes on each side. Add the cider, cover and simmer for 30 minutes, or until the pork is tender.

Meanwhile, simmer the prunes in the lemon juice and water to cover for 20 minutes, or until soft.

With a slotted spoon, transfer the meat and prunes to a warmed serving dish; keep hot. Add 3 tablespoons of the prune liquid to the skillet. Stir well and simmer until the sauce is reduced and thickened.

Stir in the currant jelly and cream and heat gently. Pour the sauce over the pork and serve immediately. Garnish with chopped parsley if desired.

Fruited Pork Chops

1 tablespoon butter
2 pork chops, about
 ¾ inch thick
Grated rind and juice
 of ½ orange
Salt and pepper
1 small onion, finely
 chopped
½ green pepper,
 seeded and
 chopped
1 cup stock or broth
1 teaspoon
 cornstarch
Pinch of sugar
⅓ cup dried apricots

Melt the butter in a small skillet. Add the chops and brown on both sides until evenly done.

With a slotted spoon, transfer to a shallow baking dish. Sprinkle with the orange rind and season with salt and pepper.

Add the onion and green pepper to the skillet and sauté until soft. Add the stock. Stir the cornstarch into the orange juice and add to the skillet. Heat, stirring, until the sauce thickens. Add the sugar and salt and pepper to taste.

Arrange the apricots on top of the pork and pour the sauce over the top. Cover with foil and bake in a 350° oven for 1 to 1¼ hours. Serve garnished with watercress if desired.

23

Glazed Ham with Apricots

4 to 6 dried apricots
½ teaspoon prepared
  mustard
1 teaspoon honey
Pepper
2 ham steaks, about
  ½ lb each
2 teaspoons
  cornstarch
1 teaspoon instant
  chicken bouillon

Place the apricots in a bowl and cover with cold water. Soak for 2 to 3 hours.

Combine the mustard, honey and pepper to taste. Spread this mixture over both sides of the ham steaks. Broil for 6 to 8 minutes on each side.

Drain the apricots, reserving the liquid; if necessary, add enough water to make ⅔ cup. Blend the cornstarch with some of the liquid, then stir in the remaining liquid.

Pour into a saucepan and cook, stirring, until the sauce becomes thick. Add the bouillon and apricots and simmer for 1 minute; adjust the seasoning.

Serve the ham steaks on a warmed platter and cover with sauce. Garnish with parsley sprigs if desired.

Sausage and Blackeye Peas Casserole

¼ cup dried blackeye peas
¾ lb pork sausage links
1 small onion, finely chopped
1 can (8 oz) tomatoes
¼ cup water
1 beef bouillon cube, crumbled
½ teaspoon dried mixed herbs
Salt and pepper

Place the blackeye peas in a bowl, cover with cold water and let soak overnight. Drain, rinse and put in a saucepan. Cover with fresh cold water, bring to a boil and let simmer for 45 minutes, or until tender. Drain thoroughly and set aside.

Broil the sausages, turning often, until evenly browned. Cool slightly, then cut into ½-inch pieces. Place in a 1½-quart casserole.

Add the blackeye peas, onion, tomatoes with their liquid, water, bouillon cube and herbs to the casserole. Season with salt and pepper and mix well but gently to avoid crushing the peas.

Cover and bake in a 350° oven for 45 minutes. A crisp green salad is a good accompaniment for this dish.

Veal Marengo

1 tablespoon oil
¾ lb cubed stewing
   veal
1 clove garlic,
   crushed
1 small onion, sliced
1 tomato, peeled and
   chopped
1 cup chicken stock
   or broth
Bouquet garni
Salt and pepper
12 button
   mushrooms

Heat the oil in a skillet, add the veal and brown on all sides. Add the garlic and onion and sauté until soft.

Stir in the tomato and stock and bring to a boil. Transfer the contents of the skillet to a 1½-quart casserole and add the bouquet garni and salt and pepper to taste. Cover and bake in a 350° oven for 1¼ hours, or until the meat is almost tender.

Remove the bouquet garni and skim off any fat. Add the mushrooms and bake an additional 15 minutes. Garnish with chopped parsley if desired.

Veal with Mushrooms

2 veal cutlets, about
  ¼ inch thick
2 tablespoons butter
1 tablespoon oil
½ small onion,
  sliced
½ cup small
  mushrooms
2 tablespoons dry
  sherry
¼ cup heavy cream
Salt and pepper
Paprika
1 teaspoon chopped
  parsley

Trim the edges of the cutlets to keep the meat from curling.

Heat the butter and oil in a skillet, add the onion and sauté for 2 to 3 minutes. Add the veal and mushrooms and sauté for 8 to 10 minutes, turning the cutlets once, until golden brown on both sides.

Stir in the sherry and bring to a boil. Add the cream and heat through, stirring. Add salt and pepper to taste.

Lift the veal cutlets onto a warmed serving platter and spoon the sauce over them. Sprinkle with paprika and parsley. Garnish with a lemon twist if desired.

27

Tongue in Piquant Sauce

A deli is the answer when you feel like tongue but not like eating it for a whole week. Buy what you need and there will be no leftovers.

½ cup ketchup
2 tablespoons
  molasses
1 can (4 oz) tomato
  sauce
2 tablespoons wine
  vinegar
2 tablespoons
  brown sugar
1½ teaspoons
  cornstarch
¼ cup water
2 tablespoons
  curaçao
½ lb sliced tongue

Combine the ketchup, molasses, tomato sauce, vinegar and brown sugar in a small saucepan over low heat. Simmer, stirring constantly, until the sugar dissolves. Stir the cornstarch into the water and add to the sauce. Simmer, stirring constantly, until thickened. Stir in the curaçao and remove from the heat.

Arrange the tongue in a small shallow baking dish and pour the sauce over it. Cover and bake in a 325° oven for 25 minutes or until heated through. Garnish with parsley if desired.

Beef Liver in Sauce

4 slices bacon
1 tablespoon butter
1 small onion, chopped
2 tablespoons flour
Salt and pepper
2 slices beef or calf's liver, about ¾ lb
½ cup sliced mushrooms
⅔ cup stock or broth
1 tablespoon tomato paste
¼ teaspoon prepared mustard
2 teaspoons chutney
½ teaspoon sugar

Cook the bacon in a skillet until crisp; drain on paper towels, crumble and reserve. Melt the butter in a skillet, add the onion and sauté until soft.

Season the flour with salt and pepper and use to coat the liver. Add to the skillet and brown, turning, until evenly cooked. Stir in the crumbled bacon, mushrooms, stock, tomato paste, mustard, chutney and sugar. Add salt and pepper to taste. Bring to a boil, stirring, then cover and simmer for 20 minutes.

Transfer to a warmed serving platter and garnish with watercress if desired.

Sherried Chicken Livers

3 slices bacon
¼ cup flour
Salt and pepper
¾ lb chicken livers
1 small onion, chopped
1 clove garlic, crushed
1 cup beef stock or broth
1 tablespoon chopped parsley
½ cup sliced water chestnuts
¼ cup dry sherry

Cook the bacon in a skillet until crisp; drain on paper towels, crumble and reserve.

Season the flour with salt and pepper and toss with the livers. Reserve the flour and add the livers to the skillet and cook about 7 minutes, or until tender. Remove the livers and keep warm.

Add the onion and garlic to the skillet and sauté until soft. Stir in the remaining seasoned flour and cook for 1 minute. Add the beef stock and parsley and cook, stirring, until thickened.

Return the chicken livers to the skillet with the water chestnuts. Stir in the sherry and cook until heated through. Sprinkle with the bacon. Serve over hot cooked rice if desired.

Chicken Cacciatore

2 tablespoons olive oil
1 medium onion, sliced
½ clove garlic, minced
½ green pepper, seeded and cut into strips
12 button mushrooms
1 can (8 oz) tomatoes
Pinch of oregano
2 to 4 chicken parts
½ cup dry red wine
Salt and pepper

Heat half the oil in a saucepan large enough to hold the chicken and simmer the onion and garlic until soft. Add the green pepper and mushrooms and sauté 5 minutes. Add the tomatoes and oregano.

Meanwhile, in a skillet, brown the chicken in the remaining oil until golden. Transfer the chicken to the saucepan and drain off any oil in the skillet. Add the wine to the skillet and bring to a boil, scraping the pan. Add to the sauce.

Cover and simmer for 40 minutes. If the sauce is too thin, remove the chicken to a warmed platter and boil the sauce down until it is of the desired consistency. Season to taste with salt and pepper.

Serve the chicken with the sauce poured over it. Garnish with chopped parsley if desired.

Tarragon Baked Chicken

2 tablespoons oil
2 small baking potatoes, diced
1 clove garlic, minced
Salt and pepper
1 whole chicken breast, halved
¼ teaspoon tarragon
¾ cup dry white wine

Heat 1 tablespoon of the oil in a medium flameproof casserole. Add the potatoes, cover and simmer 5 to 10 minutes. Add the garlic and simmer 1 minute. Season with salt and pepper; cover and put in a 350° oven.

Heat the remaining oil in a skillet and brown the chicken breasts evenly. Transfer to the casserole and sprinkle with tarragon.

Discard any oil in the skillet and add the wine. Bring to a boil, scraping the pan, and pour over the chicken.

Cover and continue baking for 30 minutes, or until the potatoes are tender. Serve with the sauce poured over the chicken.

Chicken Curry

1 tablespoon butter
1 small onion,
  chopped
½ green pepper,
  seeded and
  chopped
1 tablespoon curry
  powder
2 tablespoons flour
1¼ cups chicken
  stock or broth
1 small apple,
  chopped
1 tablespoon
  shredded coconut
1 tablespoon sweet
  chutney
3 tablespoons golden
  raisins
Salt and pepper
2 cups cut-up cooked
  chicken
Hot cooked rice

Melt the butter in a saucepan, add the onion and green pepper and sauté until soft. Add the curry powder and flour and continue cooking for 1 minute. Gradually stir in the stock and cook, stirring, until thickened.

Stir in the apple, coconut, chutney, raisins and salt and pepper to taste. Cover and simmer for 10 minutes. Add the chicken and continue cooking for 20 minutes.

Serve over hot cooked rice and garnish with chopped parsley if desired.

Chicken in Peanut Sauce

2 tablespoons oil
2 chicken quarters
1 small onion, sliced
2 teaspoons flour
2 teaspoons creamy
  peanut butter
⅔ cup chicken stock
  or broth
½ teaspoon cumin
  seeds
Salt and pepper
1 tablespoon
  chopped peanuts
Hot cooked rice

Heat the oil in a skillet, add the chicken quarters and sauté until browned on all sides. Drain and transfer to a small casserole.

Sauté the onion in the oil remaining in the skillet until soft. Stir in the flour and peanut butter and cook for 1 minute. Gradually stir in the stock and bring to a boil. Add the cumin and season liberally with salt and pepper.

Pour the sauce over the chicken. Cover and bake in a 350° oven for 1 to 1¼ hours, or until the chicken is tender and the juices run yellow.

Sprinkle with the chopped peanuts and serve over hot cooked rice.

Chicken Maryland

2 tablespoons flour
Salt and pepper
4 chicken
  drumsticks
1 egg, beaten
3 tablespoons soft
  bread crumbs
1 tablespoon oil
2 tablespoons butter
4 slices bacon
2 bananas
1 tablespoon butter
1 can (8 oz) whole
  kernel corn

Season the flour with salt and pepper and toss with the drumsticks to coat. Dip the drumsticks into the egg, then coat with bread crumbs.

Heat the oil and butter in a skillet, add the chicken and sauté, turning, until golden in color. Reduce heat, cover and simmer gently for 15 to 20 minutes, turning occasionally, until the chicken is tender.

Meanwhile, prepare the accompaniments. Cut the bacon slices in half, roll up and thread onto a skewer. Broil for about 3 minutes. Cut the bananas lengthwise in half. Melt the butter in a small saucepan, add the bananas and cook slowly until golden. Heat the corn and drain thoroughly.

Drain the chicken and transfer to a warmed serving platter. Arrange the corn around the chicken and place the bananas and bacon rolls on top. Garnish with watercress if desired.

Chicken Salad

3 tablespoons raisins
2 cups cut-up cooked
  chicken
½ cup chopped
  celery
½ bunch watercress,
  chopped
Juice of ½ orange
⅔ cup mayonnaise
  (page 73)
Salt and pepper
Orange segments

Place the raisins in a bowl and cover with warm water. Let sit for 2 hours, then drain.

Combine the chicken in a bowl with the celery, watercress and raisins.

Mix the orange juice with the mayonnaise and add salt and pepper to taste. Stir into the chicken and mix well.

Spoon into a serving dish and top with orange segments. Garnish with watercress if desired.

Chicken Pot Pie

4 chicken parts
4 small onions
2 carrots, cut into
  large chunks
1 cup chicken broth
1 tablespoon butter
2 tablespoons flour
1 tablespoon
  chopped parsley
Salt and pepper
PASTRY:
1 cup all-purpose
  flour
Pinch of salt
2 tablespoons butter
2 tablespoons
  shortening
3 tablespoons cold
  water
1 egg, beaten

Poach the chicken with the onions and carrots for 15 minutes in the chicken broth. Skin and bone the chicken, tear into generous morsels and place in a shallow 2-quart casserole with the onions and carrots. Melt the butter in a small skillet and stir in the flour. Gradually add the chicken broth, stirring, and season with parsley and salt and pepper to taste. Pour the sauce over the chicken.

PASTRY: Combine the flour and salt in a bowl. Cut in the butter and shortening until the mixture resembles fine bread crumbs. Add the water and mix to a firm dough. Knead lightly, then chill for 15 minutes.

Roll out on a floured surface to a shape 1½ inches larger than the top of the casserole. Cut a 1-inch strip from the edge of the pastry and place on the dampened rim of the casserole. Brush with water and place the pastry in position, making a hole in the center. Seal, trim and flute the edge. Decorate with leaves made from the trimmings.

Brush with egg and bake in a 400° oven for 20 to 30 minutes. Serve hot.

35

Arroz con Pollo

2 to 4 chicken parts
Salt and pepper
1 tablespoon oil
1 clove garlic,
  minced
1 medium onion,
  chopped
½ cup rice
½ cup chicken stock
  or broth
½ cup tomato sauce
Pinch of saffron
1 package (9 oz)
  frozen artichoke
  hearts, thawed
1 pimiento, cut into
  strips

Season the chicken parts with salt and pepper. Heat the oil in a skillet and brown the chicken. Transfer with a slotted spoon to a shallow casserole.

Sauté the garlic and onion in the fat remaining in the skillet until soft. Add the rice and cook, stirring, until opaque. Spoon into the casserole.

Add the chicken stock and tomato sauce to the skillet and bring to a boil, scraping the pan. Add the saffron and pour the liquid into the casserole.

Cover and bake in a 350° oven for 25 minutes. Add the artichoke hearts and additional stock if necessary; arrange the pimientos on top. Cover and bake 10 minutes longer.

Braised Turkey Legs

2 turkey drumsticks,
about 1½ lb
2 tablespoons water
2 tablespoons butter
4 tablespoons
packaged stuffing
1 tablespoon
chopped parsley
Salt and pepper
1 cup chicken broth
1 teaspoon
cornstarch
dissolved in 2
tablespoons water

With a small sharp knife, free the flesh around the large end of each drumstick. Make a light incision around the base, cutting the skin. Using a paper towel for a firmer grip, pull the tendons out of the leg. Cut against the bone from the large end until the bone can be pulled free.

Heat the water and 1 tablespoon of the butter together and toss with the stuffing and parsley and salt and pepper to taste. Fill each drumstick with stuffing; skewer to hold.

Melt the remaining butter in a skillet and brown the meat. Place in a 1-quart casserole and add the broth. Cover and bake in a 350° oven for about 1 hour, or until tender.

Remove the stuffed legs to a platter; remove the skewers. Pour the juices into a saucepan over high heat. Add cornstarch and boil until slightly thickened. Served poured over the legs.

37

Turkey Piccata

½ lb turkey cutlet,
   cut into ⅛-inch
   slices
Flour
2 tablespoons butter
½ to ¾ cup dry
   white wine
1 to 2 tablespoons
   lemon juice
Salt and pepper

Pound the turkey slices gently with the side of a chef's knife or a meat pounder. Dust with flour.

Melt the butter in a skillet and sauté the turkey for about 3 minutes, or until the edges turn white. Turn and cook for the same amount of time on the second side.

Remove the turkey and add the wine. Bring to a boil, scraping the pan. Season the sauce to taste with lemon juice and salt and pepper.

Return the turkey to the skillet. Simmer 2 minutes, or until cooked through. Serve hot. Garnish with lemon peel and chopped parsley if desired.

Turkey Fricassee

1 small onion,
   chopped
1 small carrot, grated
1 stalk celery,
   chopped
⅔ cup turkey or
   chicken stock
Bouquet garni
⅔ cup milk
   (approximately)
1 tablespoon butter
2 tablespoons flour
Grated nutmeg
Salt and pepper
2 cups cut-up cooked
   turkey
1 tablespoon light
   cream

Put the onion, carrot, celery, stock and bouquet garni in a saucepan. Bring to a boil, cover and simmer for 15 minutes.

Strain the stock into a measuring cup, reserving the vegetables, and add enough milk to make 1¼ cups liquid.

Melt the butter in a separate saucepan, stir in flour and cook for 1 minute. Gradually stir in the liquid and cook, stirring, until thickened. Add nutmeg and salt and pepper to taste.

Stir in the vegetables and turkey. Cover and simmer for 15 minutes. Remove from heat and stir in the cream. Transfer to warmed dishes and serve. Sprinkle with chopped parsley if desired.

NOTE: Canned chicken broth can be used as a substitute for the turkey or chicken stock.

FISH

Sole with Applesauce

2 sole fillets, about
   5 oz each
Seasoned flour
1 egg, beaten
Dry bread crumbs
2 tablespoons butter
½ cup applesauce
Lemon juice
Prepared
   horseradish

Coat the fillets with the flour, dip in the egg and then in the crumbs.

Melt the butter in a skillet and brown the fish until golden on both sides.

Meanwhile, season the applesauce with lemon juice and horseradish to taste. Simmer in a small saucepan to heat through.

Place the fillets on a warmed dish and serve with the sauce poured over them.

Haddock with Sour Cream

¾ lb haddock fillets
Salt and pepper
3 tablespoons butter
¼ cup water
½ cup sliced
   mushrooms
½ cup sour cream
¼ teaspoon paprika
Salt and pepper

Put the haddock in a small shallow baking pan. Sprinkle with salt and pepper, dot with 2 tablespoons butter and add the water. Cover with foil and bake in a 325° oven for 20 minutes.

Melt the remaining 1 tablespoon butter in a small saucepan, add the mushrooms and sauté for 1 minute. Stir in the sour cream, paprika and salt and pepper to taste. Heat through.

Drain the fish and transfer to a warmed serving platter. Pour the sauce over the fish and serve. Garnish with parsley if desired.

Fish with Watercress Sauce

2 halibut steaks,
  about 6 oz each
1 small onion, sliced
1 bay leaf
4 black peppercorns
Grated rind of ½
  lemon
3 tablespoons cider
Salt and pepper
SAUCE:
Fish cooking liquor
2 teaspoons
  cornstarch
1 teaspoon lemon
  juice
1 egg yolk
¼ cup milk
½ bunch watercress,
  finely chopped

Place the fish in a small shallow baking dish. Add the onion, bay leaf, peppercorns, lemon rind and cider. Season with salt and pepper. Cover with foil and bake in a 325° oven for 20 minutes.

Transfer the fish to a warmed serving platter and remove the skin and bones. Keep hot.

SAUCE: Strain the fish cooking liquor and add enough water to make ⅓ cup. Blend the cornstarch with the fish liquor and lemon juice. Heat, stirring, until the sauce thickens. Beat the egg yolk with the milk and stir into the sauce. Add the watercress and salt and pepper to taste. Heat slowly; do not boil. Pour the sauce over the fish and serve immediately.

Potato Cod Bake

1 cod fillet (¾ lb)
½ small onion,
  finely chopped
1 apple, peeled and
  sliced
¼ cup cider
¼ teaspoon dried
  thyme
3 black peppercorns
¼ cup milk
  (approximately)
1 tablespoon butter
2 tablespoons flour
Salt and pepper
TOPPING:
1½ cups water
½ cup milk
2 tablespoons butter
1 package (3¼ oz)
  instant mashed
  potato flakes
Grated nutmeg
Salt and pepper

Put the cod, onion and apple in a buttered small baking dish and sprinkle with the cider, thyme and peppercorns. Cover and bake in a 325° oven for 20 minutes.

Strain the fish cooking liquor into a measuring cup and add enough milk to make ¾ cup. Melt the butter in a saucepan and stir in the flour. Cook for 1 minute, then gradually stir in the fish liquor. Simmer, stirring, until the sauce thickens. Add salt and pepper.

Flake the fish and add it to the sauce with the onion and apple. Warm through over low heat, then pour into the baking dish.

TOPPING: Bring the water, milk and butter to a boil. Remove from the heat and stir in potato flakes. Season with nutmeg, salt and pepper.

Spread the potatoes over the fish and score with a fork. Brown under a preheated broiler for 2 to 3 minutes.

Herbed Fish Cakes

2 medium potatoes,
    chopped
1 small onion, sliced
2 tablespoons milk
1 tablespoon butter
¾ lb sole or cod fillet
2 teaspoons chopped
    parsley
½ teaspoon dried
    Italian seasoning
1 egg, separated
Salt and pepper
Dry bread crumbs
2 tablespoons oil

Cook the potatoes and onion in boiling salted water until soft. Drain and mash, then beat in the milk.

Melt the butter in a skillet, add the fish and sauté until it flakes with a fork. Flake the fish and add to the potatoes. Stir in the herbs, egg yolk and salt and pepper to taste. Mix well, then allow to cool.

On a floured surface, divide the mixture into 4 parts and shape each into a flat cake. Dip the fish cakes into the egg white, then coat with bread crumbs.

Heat the oil in a skillet and sauté the fish cakes until crisp and golden on both sides. Transfer to a warmed dish. Garnish with parsley if desired.

Tuna Vol-au-Vent

1 sheet (½ of a
   17¼-oz pkg)
   frozen puff pastry,
   thawed
1½ tablespoons
   butter
1 small onion,
   chopped
1½ tablespoons
   flour
¾ cup milk
½ teaspoon Dijon
   mustard
½ cup grated Swiss
   cheese
1 can (7 oz) tuna,
   drained and flaked
1 tablespoon
   chopped parsley
Salt and pepper

Roll out the pastry dough to a 7-inch round. Score a circle in the center using a 3½-inch cookie cutter, cutting halfway through the dough.

Place the round on a cookie sheet and bake in a 425° oven for 15 to 18 minutes, or until risen and golden brown.

Meanwhile, melt the butter in a small saucepan. Add the onion and sauté until softened. Stir in the flour and cook for 1 minute. Gradually stir in the milk. Simmer, stirring, until thickened. Remove the pan from the heat and add the mustard and cheese, stirring until the cheese has melted. Add the tuna, parsley and salt and pepper to taste; stir well.

Carefully remove the lid from the vol-au-vent and set aside. Discard any soft pastry in the center, making a deep well. Fill the well with the tuna mixture and replace the lid. Serve immediately.

Crisp Baked Fish Fillets

1 tablespoon butter
2 tablespoons flour
¾ cup milk
1 tablespoon
    mayonnaise (page
    71)
½ teaspoon lemon
    juice
Salt and pepper
1 white fish fillet
    (½ lb)
⅓ cup dry bread
    crumbs
4 slices bacon,
    cooked and
    crumbled
¼ cup grated
    Cheddar cheese
Tomato slices

Melt the butter in a saucepan, stir in
the flour and simmer for 1 minute.
Gradually stir in the milk and simmer,
stirring, until the sauce thickens. Stir
in the mayonnaise, lemon juice and
salt and pepper to taste.

Place the fish in a small shallow
baking dish and pour the sauce over it.
Combine the bread crumbs, bacon and
cheese and sprinkle over the sauce.

Bake in a 375° oven for 20 minutes,
then brown under a preheated broiler
for 2 to 3 minutes. Top with tomato
slices and serve immediately.

EGG & CHEESE DISHES

Tuna and Egg Bake

1 can (3½ oz) tuna,
  drained and flaked
¼ cup frozen whole
  kernel corn
2 hard-cooked eggs,
  chopped
1 tablespoon butter
2 tablespoons flour
¾ cup milk
½ cup grated
  Cheddar cheese
2 teaspoons chopped
  chives
Salt and pepper
½ cup crushed
  potato chips

Put the tuna in a small shallow baking dish and top with the corn and eggs.

Melt the butter in a saucepan, stir in the flour and simmer for 1 minute. Gradually stir in the milk and simmer, stirring, until the sauce thickens. Add the cheese, chives and salt and pepper to taste. Pour the sauce over the fish and sprinkle with the potato chips. Bake in a 350° oven for 30 minutes. Garnish with chopped chives if desired.

Farmhouse Omelet

1 tablespoon butter
1 onion, chopped
1 potato, diced
2 slices bacon,
   chopped
¼ cup chopped
   mushrooms
3 eggs
2 tablespoons milk
¼ teaspoon dried
   mixed herbs
Salt and pepper
½ cup grated
   Cheddar cheese

Melt the butter in a medium skillet, add the onion, potato and bacon and simmer until soft. Add the mushrooms, increase the heat and cook until the vegetables begin to brown.

Beat the eggs, milk and herbs and season with salt and pepper. Pour over the vegetables, tilting the skillet to spread the mixture evenly. Cook over moderate heat until the omelet starts to set.

Sprinkle with the cheese and put the skillet under a preheated broiler, keeping the door slightly ajar. Cook until the cheese is bubbling and golden brown.

Sprinkle with parsley and cut the omelet in half. Serve on warmed plates.

Pipérade

4 tablespoons butter
1 clove garlic, crushed
1 onion, chopped
1 green pepper, seeded and thinly sliced
3 tomatoes, peeled, seeded and chopped
Salt and pepper
4 eggs
1 teaspoon chopped parsley

Melt half the butter in a saucepan, add the garlic and vegetables and sauté gently until soft but not browned. Season with salt and pepper.

Lightly whisk the eggs with the parsley. Heat the remaining butter in a preheated 8-inch omelet pan over high heat until sizzling. Pour in the eggs and cook until just beginning to set, then quickly stir in the vegetables. Lower the heat and continue cooking, without stirring, until eggs are set. Slide unfolded onto a warmed dish and serve immediately.

Omelet Lorraine

3 eggs
Salt and pepper
1 package (2 oz) smoked ham, shredded
½ cup grated Gruyère cheese
1 tablespoon butter

Lightly whisk the eggs with salt and pepper and stir in half the ham and cheese.

Melt the butter in a preheated 8-inch omelet pan until it sizzles. Pour in the eggs and cook until beginning to set but still soft in the center.

Sprinkle the remaining ham and cheese over the eggs and fold the omelet in half. Turn onto a warmed serving dish and serve. Garnish with watercress if desired.

Fish Omelet

4 eggs
¼ cup milk
Salt and pepper
2 tablespoons butter
1 onion, chopped
4 tomatoes, sliced
½ cup flaked cooked white fish
1 tablespoon chopped chives

Whisk the eggs lightly with the milk and a little salt and pepper.

Melt the butter in a preheated 8-inch omelet pan until sizzling. Add the egg mixture and cook slowly. While the top is still soft, cover with the onion, tomatoes and fish. When just set, sprinkle with chives. Slide unfolded onto a warmed serving plate. Serve immediately.

Cheese-Topped Sandwiches

4 slices bacon, cut up
½ cup sliced
  mushrooms
2 tomatoes, peeled
  and chopped
½ teaspoon prepared
  mustard
Salt and pepper
2 tablespoons butter
4 slices whole wheat
  bread
½ cup grated
  Cheddar cheese

Partially cook the bacon in a skillet. Add the mushrooms and tomatoes and cook for 1 minute. Stir in the mustard and salt and pepper to taste.

Butter the bread. Spread the bacon mixture on two of the bread slices and top with the remaining two slices. Toast both sides of the sandwiches under a preheated broiler until golden brown.

Sprinkle the cheese on top and return to the broiler. Broil until the cheese is golden and bubbling. Serve immediately. Garnish with parsley if desired.

Biscuit Pizzas

1 cup all-purpose
  flour
1 teaspoon baking
  powder
½ teaspoon salt
Pinch of dry mustard
2 tablespoons butter
6 tablespoons milk
TOPPING:
1 can (16 oz)
  tomatoes, drained
  and chopped
2 tablespoons grated
  onion
¼ teaspoon dried
  oregano
¼ teaspoon dried
  basil
Salt and pepper
2 slices salami, cut
  up
1 cup grated
  mozzarella cheese
6 stuffed olives,
  sliced

Combine the flour with the baking powder, salt and mustard in a bowl. Cut in the butter until the mixture resembles fine bread crumbs. Stir in the milk and mix to a firm dough. Place on a floured surface and knead until smooth.

Divide the dough in half. Roll out each piece to a 6- to 7-inch round and put on a greased cookie sheet.

TOPPING: Arrange the tomatoes on the rounds and sprinkle with the onion, herbs and salt and pepper. Sprinkle the salami and mozzarella cheese over the pizzas and top with the olives.

Bake in a 400° oven for 15 to 20 minutes, or until the cheese is brown and bubbling. Serve warm, with a mixed salad.

Cheese Fondue

1 clove garlic, cut in half
1 tablespoon butter
6 tablespoons dry white wine
1 cup grated Cheddar cheese
1 cup grated Swiss cheese
1 teaspoon cornstarch
1 tablespoon brandy
Grated nutmeg
Pepper
French bread, cut into cubes

Rub the inside of an earthenware fondue pot or flameproof casserole with the cut garlic clove. Add the butter and wine and heat slowly. Add the cheeses and cook slowly, stirring, until melted.

Blend the cornstarch and brandy, making a smooth paste and stir into the fondue. Season to taste with nutmeg and pepper. Continue to cook for 3 to 4 minutes, or until the mixture is smooth and creamy.

To serve, keep the fondue warm at the table. Put cubed bread on a serving plate. Each person spears a piece of bread with a long-handled fondue fork and dips it into the fondue. Serve with a green salad.

Scotch Woodcock

4 slices hot toast,
  buttered
Anchovy paste
2 tablespoons butter
3 to 4 eggs, beaten

Spread the toast with anchovy paste. Melt the butter in a small skillet and cook the eggs over low heat, stirring, until lightly scrambled. Spoon onto the toast and serve. Garnish with watercress if desired.

Welsh Rarebit

1 cup grated Cheddar
  cheese
⅓ cup beer or ale
1 egg yolk
1 tablespoon butter
Pinch each salt and
  pepper
Dash of Worcester-
  shire sauce
2 slices bread,
  toasted
Cayenne pepper

Combine all ingredients except the toast and cayenne pepper in a heavy saucepan. Heat slowly, stirring occasionally, until smooth, creamy and hot; *do not boil*.

Place the toast on warmed serving plates. Pour the cheese mixture over the toast, sprinkle with cayenne pepper and serve immediately.

Golden Buck Rarebit: Use 1 whole egg instead of the yolk. Use flameproof plates and brown under a preheated very hot broiler for 1 minute before serving.

Swiss Rarebit: Use Gruyère cheese instead of the Cheddar, light cream instead of beer and grated nutmeg instead of Worcestershire.

Grilled Cheese Special

2 slices bread,
  buttered
4 slices Cheddar
  cheese
2 tomatoes, sliced
2 slices bacon, cut in
  half
2 fried eggs

Place the bread, buttered sides up, in a shallow flameproof dish and toast under a preheated hot broiler until golden brown. Cover completely with the cheese and broil until just melted.

Place the tomatoes on top of the cheese and cover with the bacon. Broil until the bacon is crisp. Top each slice with a fried egg and serve immediately.

Eggs Florentine

1 package (10 oz)
  frozen chopped
  spinach, thawed
Salt and pepper
2 to 4 poached eggs
2 tablespoons butter
2 tablespoons flour
1 cup milk or
  half-and-half
1½ cups grated
  Cheddar cheese

Line two ramekins with spinach. Season with salt and pepper. Slip the eggs onto the spinach.

Melt the butter in a saucepan and stir in the flour. Gradually stir in the milk and simmer, stirring, until thickened. Lower the heat, add two-thirds of the cheese and stir until melted. Pour the mixture over the eggs and sprinkle with the remaining cheese.

Bake on the top rack of a 400° oven for 15 to 20 minutes, or until golden brown. Serve immediately.

Eggs Mornay: Omit the spinach and add ⅓ cup fine fresh bread crumbs to the cheese used for the topping.

54

Eggs Flamenco

1 tablespoon oil
2 tablespoons butter
1 potato, cooked and
  diced
¼ lb precooked
  Polish sausage,
  chopped
1 sweet red pepper,
  seeded and
  shredded
2 tomatoes,
  quartered
1 tablespoon
  chopped parsley
2 eggs
4 tablespoons light
  cream
Cayenne pepper

Heat the oil and butter in a skillet, add the potatoes and sausage and sauté quickly until lightly browned, shaking the pan to keep the potatoes from sticking. Add the pepper and tomatoes and simmer for 3 to 4 minutes.

Remove from heat, stir in the parsley and season with salt and pepper. Transfer to 1 large buttered ovenproof dish. Break the eggs on top and season with salt and pepper.

Bake in a 325° oven for 15 to 20 minutes, until the eggs have set.

Pour over the cream and lightly sprinkle with cayenne. Serve hot, with crusty bread.

Blue Cheese Cauliflower

1 small cauliflower,
   cut into flowerets
1 tablespoon butter
2 tablespoons flour
¾ cup milk
½ cup crumbled
   blue cheese
Salt and pepper
1 tablespoon dry
   bread crumbs

Cook the cauliflower in boiling salted water until tender, about 10 minutes. Drain and transfer to a warmed flameproof serving dish.

Melt the butter in a saucepan, stir in the flour and cook for 1 minute. Gradually stir in the milk and simmer, stirring until thickened.

Stir in the cheese and heat slowly, stirring, until melted. Add salt and pepper to taste.

Pour the sauce over the cauliflower and top with the bread crumbs. Brown under a preheated broiler. Serve hot.

Caraway Cabbage

3 cups shredded red
  or white cabbage
1 small onion,
  chopped
½ teaspoon caraway
  seeds
1 tablespoon butter,
  melted
½ sweet red pepper,
  seeded and sliced
Salt and pepper

Cook the cabbage, onion and caraway seeds in boiling salted water for 5 to 8 minutes, or until just tender. Drain and return to the pan.

Add the butter and red pepper and toss the ingredients over low heat for 1 minute. Add salt and pepper and transfer to a warmed serving dish. Serve immediately.

Vegetarian Stew

¼ cup dried chick
   peas
¼ cup dried navy
   beans
¼ cup dried
   blackeye peas
¼ cup dried red
   kidney beans
1 tablespoon butter
1 small onion,
   chopped
1 carrot, sliced
1 stalk celery,
   chopped
1 clove garlic,
   crushed
1 can (8 oz) tomatoes
½ teaspoon dried
   Italian seasoning
Salt and pepper
½ cup grated
   Parmesan cheese

Place the chick peas, navy beans and blackeye peas in a bowl and cover with cold water. Place the kidney beans in a separate bowl and cover with cold water. Soak overnight.

Drain and place the chick peas, navy beans and blackeye peas in a saucepan; put the kidney beans in a separate pan (to keep the other beans from turning pink). Cover the peas and beans with fresh cold water. Bring to a boil and boil for 10 minutes. Cover and simmer for 40 minutes, or until the peas and beans are tender. Rinse under cold water and drain thoroughly.

Melt the butter in a saucepan, add the onion, carrot and celery and sauté until soft. Stir in the garlic, peas, beans, tomatoes with their juice and the Italian seasoning.

Bring to a boil, cover and simmer for 1 to 1¼ hours, adding water if the mixture becomes too dry. Add salt and pepper to taste. Transfer to a warmed dish; serve immediately, sprinkled with the Parmesan cheese.

Vegetables with Rice

½ cup uncooked
  brown rice
1 tablespoon oil
2 leeks, sliced
1 carrot, thinly
  sliced
1 onion, sliced
½ apple, chopped
½ teaspoon cumin
  seeds
½ teaspoon ground
  coriander
Pinch of cayenne
  pepper
4 to 5 tablespoons
  stock or broth
Salt and pepper

Cook the rice in 1¼ cups boiling salted water for 45 to 50 minutes, or until tender.

Meanwhile, heat the oil in a saucepan, add the leeks, carrot, onion and apple and sauté, stirring, for 3 minutes. Add the spices and continue cooking for 3 minutes. Stir in the stock, cover and simmer for 10 to 15 minutes, or until the vegetables are tender. Season to taste with salt and pepper.

Stir the rice into the vegetables and cook slowly for 5 minutes. Transfer to a warmed dish. Garnish with parsley if desired.

Ratatouille

1 small eggplant
Salt and pepper
1½ tablespoons
  olive oil
1 small onion, sliced
1 clove garlic,
  crushed
1 stalk celery,
  chopped
½ green pepper,
  seeded and
  chopped
2 tomatoes, peeled
  and chopped
2 tablespoons water
½ teaspoon dried
  oregano
½ teaspoon dried
  basil

Cut the eggplant into thin slices and sprinkle with salt. Place in a colander and let stand for 30 minutes. Rinse and pat dry with paper towels.

Heat the oil in a skillet and add eggplant, onion, garlic, celery and green pepper. Cook, stirring, until the vegetables are coated with oil. Cover and simmer for 10 minutes.

Add the tomatoes, water, oregano and basil. Bring to a boil, cover and simmer for 30 minutes. Season to taste with salt and pepper.

Serve hot or cold, garnished with chopped parsley if desired.

60

Minted Zucchini Mix

½ lb zucchini, thinly sliced
½ cup frozen peas
½ cup frozen whole kernel corn
2 mint sprigs
1 tablespoon butter
2 teaspoons chopped chives

Put the zucchini in a saucepan with boiling salted water. Add the peas, corn and mint. Cover and simmer for 5 minutes, or until the vegetables are just tender.

Drain thoroughly, discard the mint sprigs and return the vegetables to the saucepan.

Add the butter and chives and toss over low heat for 1 minute. Transfer the mixture to a warmed serving dish and serve hot.

French-Style Peas

1 package (10 oz)
  frozen peas
3 lettuce leaves,
  shredded
2 tablespoons butter
3 green onions,
  finely chopped
½ teaspoon sugar
¼ cup chicken stock
  or broth
1 sprig each parsley
  and mint, tied
  together
Salt and pepper

Combine the ingredients in a saucepan, seasoning with salt and pepper. Slowly bring to a boil, cover and simmer for 10 to 12 minutes, or until the peas are tender; add more stock or water as needed.

Discard the parsley and mint and transfer the contents of the saucepan to a warmed serving dish.

Potatoes with Sour Cream

3 medium potatoes,
  thinly sliced
1 small onion, finely
  chopped
¼ cup sour cream
Salt and pepper
3 tablespoons butter
⅓ cup milk

Place a layer of potatoes in the bottom of a greased shallow baking dish. Add a little of the onion and sour cream, then season with salt and pepper. Repeat the layers, ending with a layer of the potatoes.

Melt 2 tablespoons of the butter in a saucepan, stir in the milk and pour over the potatoes. Dot with the remaining butter.

Cover and bake in a 375° oven for 45 minutes. Uncover and bake for 20 minutes longer, or until the potatoes are tender and golden brown.

Garnish with chives if desired. Excellent with lamb chops or ham.

Baked Zucchini

1 tablespoon butter
1 small onion,
  chopped
½ lb zucchini, sliced
1 large tomato,
  sliced
½ teaspoon dried
  oregano
Salt and pepper
1 egg, beaten
½ cup grated
  Gruyère cheese

Melt the butter in a saucepan, add the onion and sliced zucchini and sauté for 2 minutes. Transfer to a small shallow baking dish and arrange the tomato on top. Sprinkle with the oregano and salt and pepper.

Combine the egg and cheese and spoon over the tomatoes. Bake in a 350° oven for 15 to 20 minutes, or until the top is golden brown.

Stuffed Peppers

2 medium green
  peppers
1 tablespoon butter
½ small onion,
  finely chopped
1 cup cooked rice
2 slices bacon, cooked
  and crumbled
½ cup grated
  Cheddar cheese
¼ cup light cream
¼ teaspoon prepared
  mustard
1 teaspoon chopped
  parsley
1 teaspoon chopped
  basil (optional)
Grated nutmeg
Salt and pepper

Cut the tops from the peppers and reserve; remove the seeds and membranes. Blanch the peppers in boiling salted water for 2 minutes. Drain.

Melt the butter in a saucepan, add the onion and sauté until soft. Remove from the heat and stir in the rice, bacon and cheese.

Beat the cream with the mustard, parsley, basil and nutmeg and season with salt and pepper. Stir into the rice. Spoon the mixture into the pepper shells and replace the tops.

Place in a shallow baking dish, cover with foil and bake in a 350° oven for 15 to 20 minutes. Serve hot.

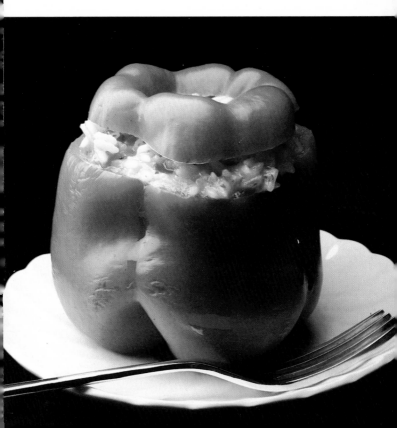

Bean Sprout Salad

¼ lb bean sprouts
1 stalk celery,
    chopped
1 carrot, grated
1-inch piece
    cucumber, cut
    into julienne
    strips
3 tablespoons raisins
2 tablespoons
    French dressing
    (page 73)
1 tablespoon plain
    yogurt
Salt and pepper

Combine the bean sprouts, celery, carrot, cucumber and raisins in a bowl.

Stir the French dressing into the yogurt. Season to taste with salt and pepper. Pour the dressing over the salad and toss well. Excellent with any meat or fish.

Avocado Salad

4 slices bacon
½ avocado, peeled
  and sliced
2 teaspoons lemon
  juice
3 lettuce leaves,
  shredded
2 green onions,
  chopped
¼ cup salted peanuts
2 tablespoons
  French dressing
  (page 73)
Salt and pepper

Cook the bacon in a skillet until crisp. Drain on paper towels and crumble.

Place the avocado slices in a serving bowl and sprinkle with the lemon juice. Add the lettuce, green onions, bacon, peanuts and French dressing. Toss well and season to taste with salt and pepper. Chill before serving.

Fruit Slaw

1 red apple, diced
2 teaspoons lemon
   juice
1 cup shredded
   cabbage
1 small carrot, grated
¼ cup chopped
   pitted dates
1 tablespoon raisins
10 seedless grapes,
   halved
2 tablespoons plain
   yogurt
2 tablespoons
   mayonnaise (page
   73)
Salt and pepper

Place the apple in a bowl, sprinkle with the lemon juice and toss well. Add the cabbage, carrot, dates, raisins and grapes.

Combine the yogurt and mayonnaise and season to taste with salt and pepper. Pour the dressing over the salad and toss well. Spoon into serving bowls.

Cheese-Filled Avocado

1 avocado
1 teaspoon lemon
   juice
½ cup crumbled
   blue cheese
2 tablespoons
   small-curd cottage
   cheese
Salt and pepper

Cut the avocado in half and remove the pit. Scoop out the flesh, leaving ½-inch thick shells, and place in a bowl with the lemon juice. Reserve the shells.

Add the cheeses to the bowl and mash the mixture with a fork. Season to taste with salt and pepper. Spoon into the reserved shells and chill in the refrigerator briefly. Garnish with parsley if desired.

Bean and Pasta Salad

1½ cups pasta shells
½ cup canned red
  kidney beans,
  drained
½ green pepper,
  seeded and
  chopped
2 teaspoons chopped
  parsley
Grated rind and juice
  of ½ orange
2 tablespoons
  French dressing
  (page 73)
Salt and pepper

Cook the pasta in plenty of boiling salted water until tender but still firm to the bite. Drain and rinse under cold running water; drain again.

Place the pasta in a serving bowl. Add the kidney beans, green pepper, parsley and orange rind. Mix the orange juice with the French dressing and season to taste with salt and pepper. Pour the dressing over the salad and toss well. Serve chilled.

70

Creamy Potato Salad

½ lb new potatoes,
    cooked and cut up
Chopped watercress
    sprigs
¼ cup chopped
    cooked ham
¼ cup heavy cream
1 teaspoon prepared
    mustard
Pinch of sugar
Salt and pepper

Put the potatoes (preferably while still warm) in a bowl and add the chopped watercress and ham.

Lightly whip the cream with the mustard, sugar and salt and pepper to taste. Add to the potatoes and mix well.

Spoon into a serving dish. Refrigerate for at least 30 minutes before serving. Excellent with cold cuts.

Waldorf Salad

2 apples, diced
2 teaspoons lemon
  juice
2 stalks celery,
  chopped
¼ cup salted peanuts
¼ cup chopped
  walnuts
3 tablespoons
  mayonnaise (see
  below)

Toss the apples in a bowl with the lemon juice. Add the remaining ingredients and mix well.

Serve in a lettuce-lined bowl. Sprinkle with paprika if desired.

French Dressing

1 tablespoon Dijon
  mustard
½ teaspoon sugar
1 teaspoon each
  finely chopped
  chives and parsley
5 tablespoons wine
  vinegar
10 tablespoons olive
  oil
½ teaspoon salt
Dash of pepper

Combine the mustard, sugar and herbs in a screw-top jar. Stir in the vinegar. Add the oil and salt and pepper. Before serving, shake thoroughly to blend.
Makes about 1¼ cups

Mayonnaise

2 egg yolks
½ teaspoon salt
½ teaspoon pepper
½ teaspoon dry
  mustard
1 teaspoon sugar
1¼ cups olive oil
1½ tablespoons
  white vinegar or
  lemon juice

Make sure all ingredients are at room temperature.

Beat the egg yolks in a bowl with the salt, pepper, mustard and sugar. Add the oil, drop by drop, beating constantly. As the mayonnaise thickens, the oil may be added in a thin stream.

When all the oil has been added, gradually add the vinegar and mix thoroughly.
Makes about 1¼ cups

DESSERTS

Zabaglione

2 egg yolks
2 tablespoons sugar
2 tablespoons
   Marsala or 4
   tablespoons
   sherry

Fit a small stainless steel bowl over a pan of hot water. Whisk the egg yolks with the sugar in the bowl until the mixture begins to thicken and mound. Gradually whisk in the Marsala.

Pour into dessert glasses and serve warm. Accompany with cookies if desired.

Meringues

Meringues are a delicious and economical way of using up extra egg whites, and they can be kept for long periods if stored, loosely covered with a towel, in a dry place.

2 egg whites
Pinch of salt
Pinch of cream of
  tartar
½ cup sugar

Beat the egg whites with the salt and cream of tartar until soft peaks form. Add the sugar slowly, a tablespoon at a time, and beat until stiff.

With the back of a spoon, shape into 4 shells on a greased and floured baking sheet. Bake at 180° for 2 hours, or leave overnight in an oven with a pilot light.

Serve filled with ice cream or fruit; top with whipped cream and/or sauce. NOTE: The meringue may be dropped from a spoon or piped from a bag with a fancy tip into small shapes. Bake in the same way as above, and use to accompany other desserts.

Soufflé Omelet

Soufflé omelets are usually filled with a sweet mixture and served as a dessert. Here are 4 different suggestions for serving this special dessert.

2 eggs, separated
2 teaspoons cold
  water
2 teaspoons sugar
¼ teaspoon vanilla
1 tablespoon butter
Powdered sugar

Beat the egg yolks with the water, sugar and vanilla until pale and creamy. Beat the egg whites until stiff enough to hold peaks, then gently fold the yolk mixture into the whites.

Melt the butter in a preheated small ovenproof skillet until it begins to sizzle. Add the egg mixture and spread evenly. Cook slowly for about 2 minutes until set around the edge, then place under a preheated moderately hot broiler for 1 to 2 minutes, or until the surface feels firm to the touch and looks puffy. (Or place in a preheated 400° oven for 3 to 4 minutes.)

Fold the omelet in half and turn onto a warmed plate. Sprinkle with powdered sugar and serve immediately.

NOTE: For a richer version, fill with strawberry jam and top with whipped cream.

SWISS-STYLE
FILLING:
2 oz unsweetened
  chocolate
2 tablespoons black
  cherry jam,
  warmed
Powdered sugar

Grate the chocolate coarsely or make curls with a vegetable peeler. Slide the unfolded omelet onto a warmed serving plate. Spread with the jam and fold in half. Top with the chocolate and sprinkle lightly with powdered sugar. Serve immediately.

ITALIAN-STYLE
FILLING:
2 scoops ice cream
2 teaspoons chopped
  nuts

Slide the unfolded omelet onto a serving plate. Top with ice cream, sprinkle with the nuts and serve.

FRENCH-STYLE
FILLING:
2 tablespoons orange
  marmalade,
  warmed
2 tablespoons
  Cointreau
Grated rind of
  1 orange

While the omelet is still in the pan, spread with some of the marmalade. Fold in half and turn onto a warmed serving plate. Stir the liqueur into the remaining marmalade, warm gently and pour over the omelet. Sprinkle with the orange rind and serve.

Banana Splits

2 bananas
4 small scoops
  vanilla ice cream
¼ cup heavy cream,
  whipped
2 teaspoons chopped
  nuts
2 maraschino
  cherries
SAUCE:
1 oz semi-sweet
  chocolate
1 tablespoon warm
  water
¼ cup firmly packed
  brown sugar
1 teaspoon corn
  syrup
⅛ teaspoon vanilla

Cut the bananas lengthwise in half and place on 2 serving dishes. Top each banana with two scoops of ice cream. Spoon or pipe the whipped cream on top and decorate with the nuts and cherries.

SAUCE: Melt the chocolate with the water in a heavy saucepan over low heat. Add the brown sugar and corn syrup. Heat gently, stirring, until the sugar has dissolved. Bring to a boil and boil steadily, without stirring, for 3 to 4 minutes. Remove from the heat and stir in the vanilla.

Pour the sauce over the banana splits or serve separately.

Spicy Rice Pudding

3 tablespoons
  uncooked rice
1¼ cups milk
¼ cup firmly packed
  brown sugar
1 teaspoon finely
  grated orange rind
¼ teaspoon grated
  nutmeg
2 tablespoons raisins
1 tablespoon butter

Put the rice in a small deep baking dish. Add the remaining ingredients and stir well.

Bake in a 325° oven for 1 hour, stirring occasionally. Serve hot or cold.

Plum Tart

1 cup all-purpose
   flour
Pinch of salt
1 teaspoon sugar
6 tablespoons butter
1 egg, beaten
3/4 lb red plums,
   halved and pitted
2/3 cup water
1/4 cup sugar
2 teaspoons
   cornstarch

Combine the flour, salt and 1 teaspoon sugar in a bowl. Cut in the butter until the mixture resembles fine bread crumbs. Add the egg and mix to a smooth dough. Knead lightly, cover and chill for 30 minutes.

Roll out the dough on a floured surface and use to line a 7-inch flan ring placed on a baking sheet. Reserve the leftover dough.

Place the plums, water and 1/4 cup sugar in a saucepan. Simmer until tender. Drain, reserving the juice.

Dissolve the cornstarch in a little water. Bring the reserved juice to a boil and stir in the cornstarch. Boil until thickened. Add the plums and spoon into the pastry shell. Roll out the dough trimmings and cut into strips. Arrange the strips in a lattice pattern over the plums.

Bake in a 400° oven for 25 minutes. Cool. Transfer the tart to a serving plate and serve dusted with powdered sugar if desired.

Crème Caramel

6 tablespoons sugar
2 egg yolks
1 cup half-and-half
¼ teaspoon vanilla

Melt 4 tablespoons of the sugar in a small skillet, stirring constantly, until golden brown. Divide between 2 6-greased ovenproof cups. Swirl and allow the sugar to harden.

Beat the egg yolks with the remaining sugar. Heat the half-and-half until almost boiling and stir into the eggs with the vanilla.

Set the cups in a small pan containing about 1 inch of hot water. Bake in a 350° oven 45 to 50 minutes, or until a knife inserted in the center comes out almost clean. Cool, then refrigerate until chilled.

To serve, invert onto plates and unmold. Garnish with slivered blanched almonds if desired.

81

Chocolate-Orange Mousse

2 oz semi-sweet
  chocolate
2 tablespoons butter
Grated rind and juice
  of ½ orange
1 egg, separated
¼ cup heavy cream,
  whipped

Melt the chocolate in a bowl over hot water. Remove from the heat and add the butter, orange rind and juice and the egg yolk. Beat until smooth. Cool.

Fold in the whipped cream. Beat the egg white until stiff and fold into the chocolate mixture. Pour into serving dishes. Chill until set.

Decorate with chocolate shavings if desired.

NOTE: To make chocolate shavings, simply shave slivers from the side of a chocolate bar with a vegetable peeler.

Ginger-Nut Ice Cream

¾ cup heavy cream
1 tablespoon milk
2 tablespoons
   powdered sugar
3 tablespoons finely
   chopped preserved
   stem ginger
2 teaspoons ginger
   syrup
2 tablespoons finely
   chopped
   hazelnuts

Whip the cream and milk in a bowl. Fold in the powdered sugar. Pour into an ice cube tray, cover with foil and freeze for about 45 minutes, or until ice crystals have formed around the sides of the tray.

Spoon into a chilled bowl and beat until smooth. Stir in the ginger, syrup and hazelnuts.

Pour into the ice cube tray, cover and freeze until firm.

About 20 minutes before serving, place in the refrigerator to soften. Spoon into serving dishes. Serve with cookies if desired.

Minted Melon

½ honeydew melon
1 orange
Crushed mint leaves

Remove the seeds from the melon, scoop out the flesh and dice. Place in a bowl.

Grate the rind from the orange and add to the melon. Peel and section the orange, discarding all the pith. Add to the melon with the crushed mint. Mix well and spoon into serving dishes; chill.

Garnish with mint sprigs and serve with cream if desired.

Crunchy Apples

2 large apples, peeled
   and sliced
2 tablespoons sugar
1 teaspoon lemon
   juice
1 tablespoon water
¼ teaspoon ground
   cinnamon
2 tablespoons butter
¼ cup oatmeal
1 tablespoon brown
   sugar
¼ cup heavy cream
1 tablespoon milk
Grated chocolate

Place the apples in a saucepan with the sugar, lemon juice, water and cinnamon. Cook slowly until the apples are soft. Mash until smooth, then spoon into individual serving dishes.

Melt the butter in a small saucepan and add the oatmeal and brown sugar. Stir together over low heat until the oatmeal is browned. Cool, then spoon the mixture over the apples.

Whip the cream and milk together lightly and spoon on top. Sprinkle with the grated chocolate.

Crème Brûlée

2 egg yolks
1 cup heavy cream
Brown sugar

Beat the egg yolks until frothy. In a 2-quart pan, bring the cream to a boil and boil 1 minute. Pour the cream over the egg yolks, then return to the heat. Bring almost to a boil.

Pour the custard into a shallow flameproof dish, 5 to 6 inches in diameter. Cool, then refrigerate until chilled.

Sprinkle the top of the crème liberally with brown sugar and place under the broiler until melted. Chill. Serve plain or over fresh fruit, such as strawberries or peaches.

Soufflé Rothschild

⅓ cup mixed glacéed fruits, finely chopped
2 tablespoons brandy
6 tablespoons milk
1½ tablespoons flour
3 tablespoons granulated sugar
2 eggs, separated
1 tablespoon butter
1 teaspoon vanilla
Pinch of salt
Powdered sugar

Place the glacéed fruits in a cup and add the brandy. Allow to stand while preparing the soufflé.

In a small saucepan, gradually beat the milk into the flour. Add 2½ tablespoons of the granulated sugar and bring to a boil, stirring. Boil and stir for 30 seconds. Remove from the heat and continue stirring to partially cool and stop the cooking.

Beat in the egg yolks, one at a time, and then the butter. Strain the brandy into the mixture; add the vanilla. Scrape down the sides of the pan and place plastic wrap directly on the surface of the mixture.

Beat the egg whites with the salt until soft peaks form. Beat in the remaining 1½ teaspoons granulated sugar until stiff.

Stir a little of the egg whites into the sauce to lighten it, then pour the remaining sauce over the whites and fold in quickly but gently.

Spoon a third of the mixture into a greased 3-cup mold. Sprinkle with half of the fruit. Spoon in half of the remaining mixture and sprinkle with the last of the fruit. Spoon in the remaining soufflé mixture and place in preheated 400° oven. Reduce the heat to 375° and bake for 20 minutes. Quickly sprinkle powdered sugar on top and continue baking for 10 to 15 minutes, or until a cake tester inserted into the middle from the side of the soufflé comes out clean.

Pineapple Freeze

½ fresh pineapple
2 tablespoons water
½ cup powdered
    sugar

Cut the fruit from the pineapple, discarding the core; reserve the shell. Chop the fruit, place in a blender with the water and process until smooth. Stir in the powdered sugar.

Spoon the mixture into the reserved shell, cover and freeze until firm.

About 20 minutes before serving, remove from the freezer and place in the refrigerator to soften. Decorate with mint sprigs if desired.

Apricot and Banana Cream

⅓ cup dried apricots
2 ripe bananas, sliced
1 teaspoon lemon juice
5 tablespoons heavy cream
2 tablespoons plain yogurt
2 teaspoons honey

Place the apricots in a bowl and add enough cold water to cover. Let soak for several hours before draining well and patting dry with paper towels.

Puree the bananas in a blender with the apricots, lemon juice, cream, yogurt and honey. The mixture should be very smooth.

Spoon into serving dishes and chill before serving. Decorate with walnut halves if desired.

Caramel Pudding

1 tablespoon butter
¼ cup packed brown sugar
¾ cup scalded milk
½ cup cold milk
2 tablespoons flour
Pinch of salt
1 egg, beaten
½ teaspoon vanilla

Melt the butter in a heavy saucepan and add the brown sugar. Cook over low heat, stirring, for 5 minutes.

Add the scalded milk and cook, stirring, until the sugar is dissolved. Stir the cold milk into the flour and salt and add to the saucepan. Cook, stirring, until the mixture thickens. Mix a spoonful of the hot liquid into the egg, then return to the saucepan. Cook and stir for 3 minutes; do not boil. Add the vanilla. Cool.

Turn into serving dishes and chill. Decorate with walnut halves.

Rhubarb Cream

½ lb rhubarb, chopped
1 tablespoon water
Grated rind of ½ orange
¼ cup sugar
½ cup heavy cream, whipped
¼ cup raspberry yogurt

Place the rhubarb in a saucepan with the water, orange rind and sugar. Cook slowly until soft. Let cool, then puree in a blender.

Fold two-thirds of the whipped cream into the rhubarb with the yogurt. Spoon into serving dishes and pipe swirls of whipped cream on top. Chill before serving.

Orange Cheesecake

2 tablespoons butter
1 cup graham cracker crumbs
1 cup small-curd cottage cheese
2 tablespoons sugar
Grated rind and juice of ½ orange
½ cup heavy cream, whipped
Canned mandarin orange sections

Melt the butter and stir in the crumbs. Press the mixture onto the bottom and sides of a 7-inch quiche or flan dish. Chill in the refrigerator until firm.

Mix the cottage cheese, sugar and orange rind and juice. Gently fold in the whipped cream. Spoon the mixture into the crumb crust.

Decorate with mandarin orange sections and chill before serving.